Thank you for choosing "The Book of Wo∎
by Pretty Pine Press!

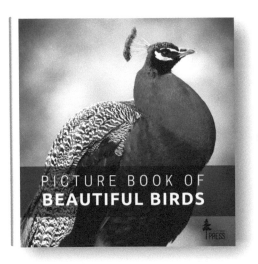

Would you like the **FREE e-BOOK: Picture Book of Beuutiful Birds?**

To claim your gift email us at prettypinepress@gmail.com

Some content taken The Holy Bible, Berean Study Bible, BSBCopyright ©2016, 2018 by Bible Hub Used by Permission. All Rights Reserved Worldwide. Scripture quotations marked (NIV) are taken from the Holy Bible, New International Version®, NIV®. Copyright © 1973, 1978, 1984, 2011 by Biblica, Inc.™ Used by permission of Zondervan. All rights reserved worldwide. www.zondervan.comThe "NIV" and "New International Version" are trademarks registered in the United States Patent and Trademark Office by Biblica, Inc.™ Some content taken from Holy Bible, New Living Translation, copyright © 1996, 2004, 2015 by Tyndale House Foundation. Used by permission of Tyndale House Publishers, Inc., Carol Stream, Illinois 60188. All rights reserved. Scripture quotations marked CSB have been taken from the Christian Standard Bible®, Copyright © 2017 by Holman Bible Publishers. Used by permission. Christian Standard Bible® and CSB® are federally registered trademarks of Holman Bible Publishers.

The LORD is my rock, my fortress and my deliverer; my God is my rock, in whom I take refuge.

He is my shield and the horn of my salvation, my stronghold.

PS 18:2
NIV

Light shines on the godly, and joy on those whose hearts are right.

PS 97:11

But you, O Lord, are a shield around me; you are my glory, the one who holds my head high.

I cried out to the Lord, and he answered me from his holy mountain.

PS 3:3-4

Know that the Lord is God. It is he who made us, and we are his; we are his people, the sheep of his pasture.

PS 100:3

NIV

Even when I go through the darkest valley, I fear no danger, for you are with me; your rod and your staff-they comfort me.

PS 23:4
CSB

Though he falls, he will not be overwhelmed, for the LORD is holding his hand.

PS 37:24

The salvation of the righteous is from the LORD; He is their stronghold in time of trouble.

PS 37:39

God is our refuge and strength, a very present help in trouble. Therefore will not we fear, though the earth be removed, and though the mountains be carried into the midst of the sea.

PS 46:1-2

Cast your burden upon the LORD and He will sustain you; He will never let the righteous be shaken.

PS 55:22

If I walk in the midst of trouble, You preserve me from the anger of my foes; You extend Your hand, and Your right hand saves me.

PS 138:7

Clouds and darkness are around him. Righteousness and justice are the foundation of his throne.

PS 97:2

He will be like a tree planted by the streams of water, that brings forth its fruit in its season, whose leaf also does not wither. Whatever he does shall prosper.

PS 1:3

The LORD is my strength and song, and is become my salvation.

PS 118:14

I have set the LORD always before me: because he is at my right hand, I shall not be moved.

PS 16:8

Be still, and know that I am God: I will be exalted among the heathen, I will be exalted in the earth.

PS 46:10

The LORD is near to the brokenhearted, And saves those who are crushed in spirit.

PS 34:18

Create in me a clean heart, O God; and renew a right spirit within me.

PS 51:10

The heavens declare the glory of God; the skies proclaim the work of His hands.

PS 19:1

You will show me the path of life. In your presence is fullness of joy. In your right hand there are pleasures forevermore.

PS 16:11

He will cover you with his feathers. Under his wings you will take refuge. His faithfulness is your shield and rampart.

PS 91:4